Making Chair Seats from Cane, Rush and Other Natural Materials

BY
RUTH B. COMSTOCK

DOVER PUBLICATIONS, INC., New York

Original text and photographs produced by Cornell Cooperative Extension, Ithaca, New York.

Published in Canada by General Publishing Company, Ltd., 30 Lesmill Road, Don Mills, Toronto, Ontario.
Published in the United Kingdom by Constable and Company, Ltd.

This Dover edition, first published in 1988, is a republication in one volume of four extension publications of the Department of Design and Environmental Analysis, New York State College of Human Ecology, a statutory college of the State University, Cornell University, Ithaca, New York: *Cornell Bulletin 681, Cane Seats for Chairs* (1981 reprint); *Cornell Bulletin 683, Rush Seats for Chairs* (1982 reprint); *Cornell Bulletin 964, Hong Kong Grass, Rope, and Twine Seats for Chairs* (1981 revision); and *Cornell Bulletin 682, Splint Seats for Chairs* (1983). The text has been completely reset and the photographs renumbered. Some text and photographs have been rearranged.

Manufactured in the United States of America
Dover Publications, Inc., 31 East 2nd Street, Mineola, N.Y. 11501

Library of Congress Cataloging-in-Publication Data

Comstock, Ruth B.
  Making chair seats from cane, rush, and other natural materials / by Ruth B. Comstock.
       p.   cm.
  "A republication of four extension publications of the Department of Design and Environmental Analysis, New York State College of Human Ecology, a statutory college of the State University, Cornell University, Ithaca, New York"—T.p. verso.
    ISBN 0-486-25693-6 (pbk.)
    1. Chair caning. I. Title.
TT199.C65 1988
684.1'3—dc19   88-15044
                                                                          CIP

CONTENTS

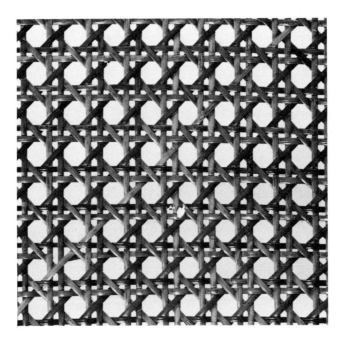

1. CANE SEATS

SELECT THE CHAIR AND CANE

Chairs with small holes drilled through the frame around the seat opening should have cane seats. If these seats are carefully woven, they will be strong and wear well.

Cane for chair seating is made from a palm called rattan. The plants come from the Indian Archipelago, China, India, Sri Lanka, and the Malay Peninsula. They grow in dense forests and frequently reach tree height; then they fall over and form a matted undergrowth. The stem, which is covered with beautiful green foliage, grows in length from 100 to 300 feet and is seldom more than 1 inch in diameter. For export, these stems are cut in 10- to 20-foot lengths. The outer bark is stripped in varying widths and packaged in amounts for one or two chairs, or in 1,000-foot hanks for four chairs with medium-sized seats. The cane is cut in pieces, preferably 6–8 feet long.

Seating cane differs from domestic sugar cane and from the cane known as bamboo, which grows in the southern states. Bamboo, which is shorter, straighter, and thicker, is used for furniture, walking sticks, poles, and the like. Neither bamboo nor sugar cane is suitable for chair seating.

You can buy cane at chair-seating and crafts-supply houses, and at certain mail-order houses and department stores. Buy long, select cane for medium or large chair seats; short lengths have to be tied more often but are usable for small seats. Good cane is smooth, glossy on the right side, tough, and pliable. The "eye," or lump where the stem of the leaf grew out, should be smooth and unbroken. Poor cane has rough and imperfect spots, does not weave easily, and is likely to split.

Plastic cane is also available. It weaves easily, does not require soaking, is strong, and costs slightly less than other cane because little is wasted (see Figure 1-39, page 9). Its smooth, shiny texture is suitable for painted chairs; real cane is preferable for fine old furniture.

Binder, to finish the edge of the seat, is cane one width wider than that used for weaving and usually is included with the weaving cane.

The width of cane to use depends on the size of the holes in the chair seat and the distance between them. The following is a guide to the size of cane to buy.

Size of cane to use

Cane size	Size of hole	Distance between holes
Superfine	3/16″	3/8″
Fine fine	3/16	1/2
Fine	3/16	5/8
Narrow medium	3/16	3/4
Medium	1/4	3/4
Common	5/16	7/8

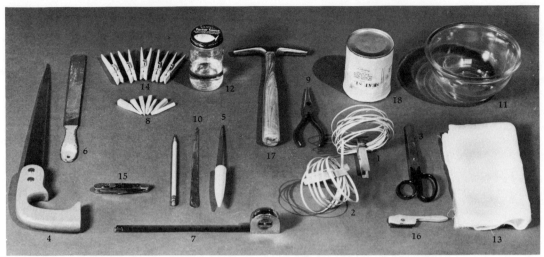

Figure 1-1—Equipment.

EQUIPMENT YOU NEED

- 1. Cane
- 2. Binder
- 3. Scissors
- 4. Keyhole saw or shears
- 5. Awl, blunt ice pick, or knitting needle
- 6. Wood file
- 7. Steel rule and a sharp pencil
- 8. Wooden pegs—whittled or cut from soft wood or ⅜" dowels, or purchased—2 dozen
- 9. Long-nose pliers
- 10. Nail file or other flat, pointed tool
- 11. Bowl, 5 to 6 inches in diameter
- 12. Glycerine, U.S.P. Standard, 3 tablespoons, or urea crystals, 2 tablespoons. Desirable but optional
- 13. Cloth or towel
- 14. Clamp clothespins, 12
- 15. Knife
- 16. Razor blade
- 17. Tack hammer
- 18. Seat stain, if desired; and cloth to apply it

PREPARE TO WEAVE

The seat

Cut away the old seat, using a keyhole saw or shears. Be careful not to mar the finish. Save the old seat as a weaving guide.

Clean any pieces of broken cane or dirt from the holes and the seat rails. Pull out old nails and tacks. Be sure you can get cane through all the holes. If any are filled, bore a hole through them.

Use a file to round the inside of the frame so no sharp edges will cut the cane.

If you need to refinish the wood, do this as far as the final coat before the seat is caned.

The cane

Pull one of the pieces of cane from the looped end of the hank, near where it is tied. As you pull, shake the hank so that the cane will not tangle or tear. Roll the piece, right side (smooth side) out, to fit in a 5- to 6-inch bowl. Fasten the ends with a clamp clothespin.

Fill the bowl with a 10 percent solution of glycerine, about 1½ tablespoons of glycerine to 1 cup of water. Soak the roll of cane in the solution. Warm water hastens the process. Or urea crystals may be used. Either solution helps to prevent the cane from drying out, but glycerine is preferable.

Let the cane soak for about 20 minutes or until it is soft and pliable.

Plastic cane, enough for one chair, is sold in a bunch with strands cut 6 to 7 yards long. If you buy it in quantity on a spool, cut it in pieces of workable length. **Do not soak it.**

HOW TO WEAVE

Square or oblong seats

The usual form of weaving is called *seven-step weaving:* Weave from the upper side of the seat; first, from back to front, then from side to side, again from back to front, and from side to side, and then on the two diagonals. If you begin in the center of the back, you will find it easy to make sure the rows of cane are straight. Add the binder last.

Step 1. Count the holes in the back rail. If there is an odd number of holes, put a peg in the center hole. If the number is even, put the peg in one of the holes nearest the center. Do the same on the front rail, pegging the same side of the center as at the back (Figure 1-2).

Take the roll of cane from the bowl and wipe off excess water with your fingers, sponge, or cloth. Put another piece in to soak while you work.

Figure 1-2

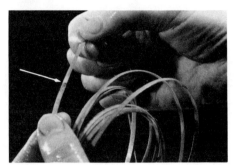

Figure 1-3

Figure 1-4

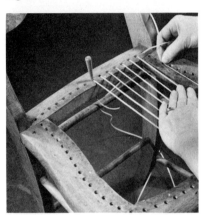

Figure 1-5

Figure 1-6

Weave with the eye whenever you can so you do not roughen or break the strand (Figure 1-3).

Pull out the peg from the back rail. Push about 4 inches of an end of cane down through this hole and fasten it with a peg.

Bring the cane to the front rail, right side up; take out the peg and push the cane through. Leave the cane slack; the mesh tightens as weaving continues. Replace the peg.

Push the cane up through the nearest hole on one side of the center. Pull it across the chair and down through the opposite hole at the back (Figure 1-4). Be sure the cane is not twisted in the hole or underneath.

As you weave, hold the cane so that it sags a little below the level of the wood seat frame (Figure 1-5). Weave large seats and plastic cane tighter. If the chair has a scoop seat, press the cane down as far as the bottom of the wood frame.

Continue weaving toward the side as long as you can weave in opposite holes. Do not use corner holes unless you are sure there will be room for the diagonal and binder canes that must also go through these holes. Leave the rest of the strand to use later. Fasten it with a clamp clothespin to keep it out of your way.

For seats wider at the front than at the back, weave separate pieces of cane as shown in Figures 1-5 and 1-6. Canes must not be carried across on the underside of the frame to block holes that will be used later.

As you continue weaving, move a peg from one hole to the next to keep the cane in place; peg ends of cane.

Weave the other half of the seat.

Step 2. Start at the back on the right side rail as you face the chair, in a hole next to the corner.

Pull the cane up through the hole and across the seat over the weaving you have already done (Figure 1-7).

Figure 1-7

Figure 1-8

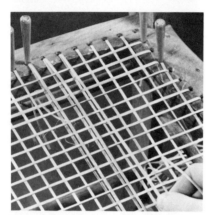

Figure 1-9

Figure 1-10

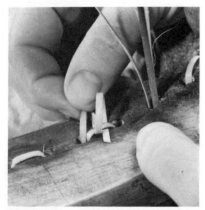

Figure 1-11

Figure 1-12

Figure 1-13

Continue weaving back and forth. If the front rail is curved, weave with separate pieces of cane (Figure 1-8).

Step 3. Weave as in step 1. Keep the strands slack as in steps 1 and 2. Weave in line with, and on top of, the first and second weaving and to the right of the cane you wove in the first step (Figure 1-9).

Fasten ends of cane: Fasten the ends of cane on the underside of the frame by tying or twisting them firmly around a nearby strap. Do not cross holes (Figures 1-10, 1-11, and 1-25, page 7). Fasten as many as you can before starting step 4 and then fasten as you go along. Moisten the ends of cane if necessary to help prevent breaking.

Step 4. Real weaving begins here, as you work from side to side. Start at the back as you face the chair and in a hole next to a corner. Weave toward you, in front of row two and weave *over* the canes on top and *under* the canes underneath (Figure 1-12). As you work, straighten the canes you wove in step 2 to help keep step-4 canes in place. When you are a third or half way across, pull the length through that far, being careful that it does not twist or break. As you pull, keep your hand level with the chair rail. If you lift up, the weaving cane may cut canes already woven, especially if the cane is plastic. Continue weaving across the row. This draws together in pairs the canes from front to back and from side to side. When you reach the opposite side, put the end of cane down through the hole and peg it until you weave the next row. Pull the cane up through the nearest hole and weave back across the seat, so the cane passes over the same canes and under the same canes as it did the first time (Figure 1-13). Weave with the end of cane as shown in Figure 1-13.

Repeat for the other rows. At the sides, be sure the

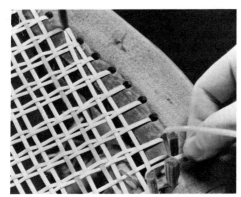

Figure 1-14

Figure 1-15

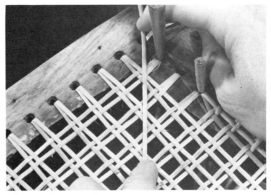

Figure 1-16

Figure 1-17

Figure 1-18

canes in step 3 are on top and at the right of canes in step 1 (Figure 1-14). Soak the woven cane with a wet sponge or cloth. Using two pegs, ice picks, or pieces of wire, straighten rows and force them together in pairs as much as you can, with hollow squares between (Figure 1-15).

Step 5. Diagonal weaving begins in this step. Start at the back corner hole on the right side as you face the chair, and weave the first row toward the left front corner. You will weave the cane diagonally *over* the pairs from front to back and *under* those from side to side, keeping the cane straight from the corner holes. First lay it in position to decide how to start (Figure 1-16). Weave with one hand on top of the seat and the other underneath, with the end of cane toward you (Figure 1-17). Pull the cane through when you have woven a few holes. Be careful not to lift it and cut the strands already woven. The cane must lie flat and be woven so the edges do not bind. The cane should pull through easily; if too wet it squeaks, if too dry moisten it with your fingers or a sponge.

Back section. Weave the back section of the seat first, using holes on the left and back rails. For the second row, weave from front to back, going over and under the same rows you did before, with the end of cane pointing away from you (Figure 1-18). As you weave, pull back on the strand and then forward to straighten diagonal canes. To decide how to start a row, plan from near the center of the seat where the pattern is established.

Weave two canes (Figure 1-19) in each corner hole to make a "fish-head" or a "V." You may complete the fish-head on the back corner or finish it when weaving

Figure 1-19

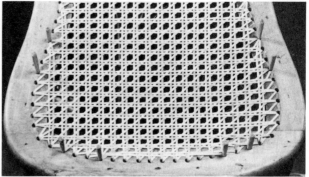
Figure 1-24

Figure 1-20

Figure 1-21

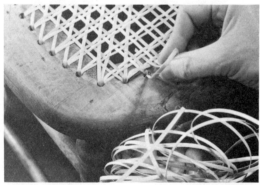
Figure 1-22

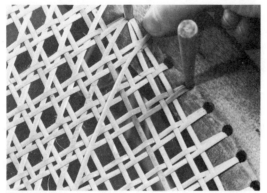
Figure 1-23

the front corner. Sometimes canes can be kept straight only by weaving a single cane in part of the corner holes. Keep the canes right side up. Do not skip holes.

Weave back and forth until you have reached a place near the center of the left side. If the seat is round or definitely curved, weave only a few diagonals and then begin to skip holes or double in holes:

Keep the rows straight. If there are more holes on the sides than on the back, skip holes, usually not more than three on the side (Figure 1-20). If the seat is round, you may double in holes across the back as well as skip holes on the side.

Make the canes lie straight across the back corner (Figure 1-21). Check to see that you have skipped enough holes so that the same number are left on the back as on the side. Use a new piece of cane when you need to, or use an end left from previous weaving if you can do so without crossing holes on the lower side of the seat. Experienced weavers use ends of cane so there will be fewer knots to tie.

The rest of the seat must be woven according to the pattern started on this section.

Front Section. Since the first diagonal was woven from back to front (Figure 1-17), weave the first row on the front section from front to back using holes on the front and right rails (Figure 1-22). Use a new piece of cane.

Check to keep the rows straight. Canes may curve slightly near the rail. Put them in holes where they will curve the least (Figure 1-23). To make the pattern alike on the two sides, weave twice (fish-head) in the hole or holes corresponding to those skipped on the left side of the chair. (Note the four pegs, two on each side, Figure 1-24). To avoid cutting the cane, you may fish-head in the hole above or below that directly opposite.

On the front rail, double in holes on the left and skip holes on the right. Note the four pegs (Figure 1-24).

Tie ends as you go along wherever there is a nearby strap to tie them to. In Figure 1-25 one end (A) is tied and the other cane out of the same hole (B) can be tied to the same strap. Those from the other hole (C) cannot be tied until more straps are formed.

Step 6. Step 6 is the second diagonal, woven in the opposite direction. Start at the back corner hole on the left side as you face the chair and weave toward the front right corner. Weave diagonally *under* the pairs from front to back and *over* those from side to side (Figure 1-26). Ends of cane should point to sides of seat.

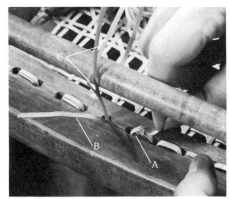

Figure 1-25

Figure 1-26

Figure 1-27

Figure 1-28

Weave the front section of the seat first. Complete the pattern started in the first diagonal, so the corners and the two sides correspond. Each half of the front and back rails should also correspond.

Front section. On the left side rail, weave twice in holes skipped by the first diagonal. Do the same on the front rail, right side. On the left side, skip those holes used twice before (Figure 1-27). Do not carry cane across holes on the underside of the seat. Instead, cut the cane if necessary.

Back section. Continue the weaving as shown in Figure 1-28. Use a new cane to weave from front to back; for this chair double in the back corner hole to match the opposite corner. Weave to the front and double in that corner hole.

On the side rail, skip holes woven in twice by the first diagonal (Figure 1-29). On the back rail, skip any holes already used twice.

Step 7. Binder cane is the next size wider than that used for weaving. It is used to cover the holes and to finish the edge of the weaving. If the seat is curved, use one strip long enough to go around. If corners are square or turns are sharp, cut separate lengths, each from 6 to 8 inches longer than the side of the seat where it will be used. Keep both binder and weaving cane wet and pliable. Lay one of the pieces of binder flat over the holes on one side of the seat with the center of the piece at about the center hole. Push one end through the corner hole and hold it there with a peg.

Use as long a piece of weaving cane as you can handle easily. Or, use a piece left from previous weaving, crossing the corner underneath if you wish. Fasten the binder at each hole (Figure 1-30) or, if the

Figure 1-29

Figure 1-30

Figure 1-31

Figure 1-32

Figure 1-33

Figure 1-34

Figure 1-35

Figure 1-36

holes are close together, at every other hole. Begin at the end where the binder is pegged. Pull the weaving cane up through the next hole, pass it over the top of the binder, and down through the same hole. Bring it up through the next hole on the same side of the binder or on alternate sides to keep the binder straight. Repeat. Both canes should be right side up, flat and tight. Use an awl or a bone knitting needle if you need to force an opening for the cane.

If a continuous piece does not lie flat around the corner, start the second side by taking out the peg and pushing the end of the binder through the corner hole. Replace the peg, hammer it tightly, and file the top level with the chair frame. Repeat around the chair. The underside of the completed seat is shown in Figure 1-31, the top in Figure 1-32.

When the cane is dry, the mesh should follow the shape of the seat frame, that is, be flat if the frame is flat and slightly curved if the frame curves.

Round seats

Round seats are more difficult and take longer to weave than do seats with straight sides. Usually fine cane is used because of the many small holes; to keep canes straight, canes often are doubled in holes. Binder canes are difficult to force through. To start weaving, count holes from seams in the seat frame.

Weaving is done as for square or oblong openings.

Figure 1-37

Figure 1-38

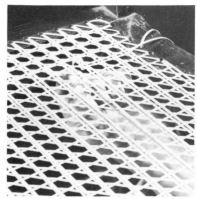

Figure 1-39

Figure 1-40

To help keep rows straight, experienced weavers may use the second diagonal as step 3.

Figure 1-33: Weave back to front (see step 1, p. 2). To keep canes in place, force a thin stick between the rails.

Figure 1-34: Weave side to side (see step 2, p. 3).

Figure 1-35: Weave the second diagonal (see step 6, p. 6). Weave *under* strand from back to front and *over* strand from side to side.

Figure 1-36: Weave back to front on top of other canes (see step 3, p. 4).

Figure 1-37: Weave side to side (see step 4, p. 4), *under* the diagonal (Figure 1-35) and the *first* strand back to front (Figure 1-33) and *over* the second strand back to front (Figure 1-36).

Figure 1-38: Complete the chair, weaving diagonally (see step 5, pp. 5 to 6), and finish with binder cane (see step 7, p. 7).

Other chairs

Plastic Cane. Plastic usually slips through easily, but edges are sharp and may cut strands already woven. Weaving is the same as for natural cane. Figure 1-39 shows the diagonal in step 6 woven as step 3 and the second cross strand *under* the diagonal *and* the *first* row from back to front.

Figure 1-40: The finished seat. (The front legs have been removed to make weaving easier and must be glued to the seat after weaving is finished.

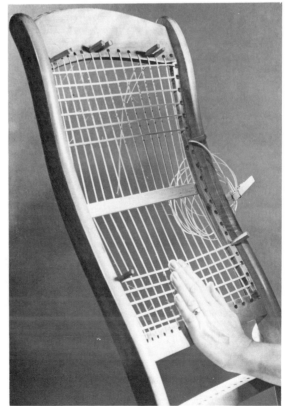

Figure 1-41

Figure 1-42

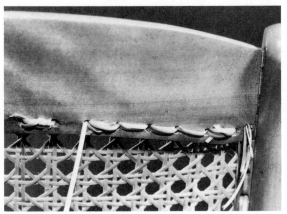

Figure 1-44

Back of Rocker. *Figure 1-41:* Weaving the back of a rocker.

Figure 1-42: Weaving a diagonal as step 3 may help hold the canes in place.

Figure 1-43: Starting the binder.

Figure 1-44: Where a strap is available, twist the ends to hold the cane instead of tying a knot.

Figure 1-45: When the binder cane is pulled tight it further holds the twisted ends in place.

Figure 1-46: In finishing the lower edge of the back, some holes have several ends of cane, and fastenings are more conspicuous.

Five-Step Weaving. *Figure 1-47:* Five-step weaving omits one row from back to front and one from side to side. *Both* diagonals are woven *under* the row from back to front and *over* the row from side to side. This makes a less sturdy seat than seven-step weaving.

HOW TO FINISH THE SEAT

Tie and cut off any loose ends on the underside of the seat. Trim off rough places or hairs with a razor blade.

Cane has a hard, glossy surface that does not need a finish. If you wish, however, you may apply a thin type of penetrating wood sealer to both sides to help prevent drying and cracking. To blend the color of a new cane seat with the finish on the chair, apply a chair-seat stain, available where you buy the cane. Rub the stain on the underside first, with a soft cloth or brush. Wipe off the surplus, and repeat on the upper side. When the stain is dry, apply a second coat if you want a darker color.

Cleaning

Cane seats can be cleaned with a cloth wrung from a solution made as follows: Place 1 quart of boiling water in the top of a double boiler (or two old basins). Add 3 tablespoons of boiled linseed oil and 1 tablespoon of turpentine. Put boiling water in the bottom of the boiler to help keep the solution hot. **Do not place the mixture directly over a flame.** Clean both sides of the seat.

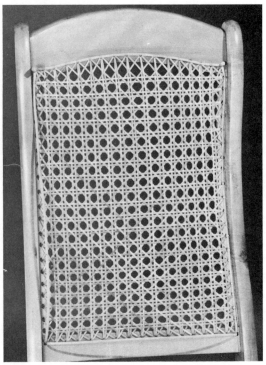

Figure 1-43

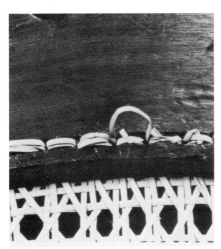

Figure 1-45

Figure 1-47

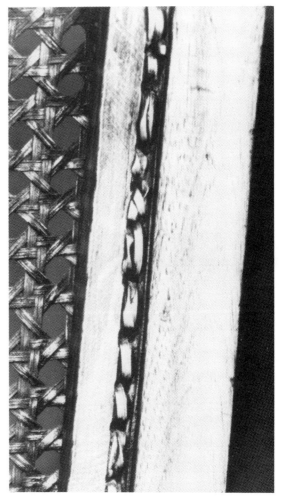

Figure 1-46

2. RUSH SEATS

Natural Rush Seats

SELECT THE CHAIR

Chairs with round rails can have seats woven either of rush or of splint; the original seat usually shows which to use. Rush can be used for chairs of simple design, such as the early American ladder-back type. It should always be chosen for more elaborate chairs, such as the later Hitchcock type and the Sheraton. Rush can be used if seat rails are of the same height, or if side rails are slightly higher than those at the front and the back.

Real rush or cattail is better than imitation fiber for antique chairs although more skill is required to weave it.

The kind of rush used for chair-seating is known as *cattail*. Cattails grow in shallow fresh water, wet swampy places, along the banks of streams, and in lowlands and marshes. They are found in most northern states and they can be gathered easily and inexpensively. If properly chosen and prepared, they are easy to use. Rush may also be bought.

HOW TO GATHER RUSH

You can tell cattails from other plants by their round spikes of flowers—the "bobs" or "cattails." The leaves are in two rows, with their flat sides back-to-back. Choose narrow, long leaves (about 7 feet) for chair seating.

Gather the rush when the leaves are full-grown, when the stalks are still green and the tips are beginning to turn brown. Late July, August, or early September is the usual time. Select perfect leaves from the stalks that do not have "bobs." Cut the stalks just above the surface of the water or ground. Gather an ample supply; leaves shrink at least one-third of their weight as they cure and there is waste in weaving.

HOW TO DRY RUSH

Pull the leaves from the stalks. Sort the leaves, placing together those of about the same width and length, and tie them in loose, flat bundles. Be careful not to bend or break the leaves. Dry them thoroughly for at least two or three weeks in a dark, airy room such as an attic or storeroom floor. Do not put the leaves in a damp room where mildew might form on the leaves, or in a hot sunny room where leaves might become brittle.

Rush carefully dried and stored should be usable for a year or more.

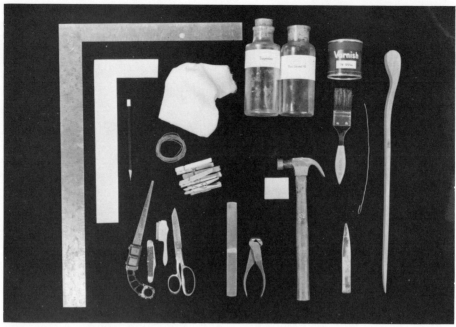

Figure 2-1—Equipment.

EQUIPMENT YOU NEED

- Chair with round rails or one with the edges of the rails rounded, with or without corner blocks
- Rush, 2½ to 3 pounds a chair
- Place where rush can be dampened, preferably a trough which can be made by soldering ends of a 6' length of 5-inch eavestrough. Or dampen in burlap with oilcloth or plastic underneath to protect the floor and cover to retain moisture
- Large teakettle or pail, about 10-quart size, and warm water
- Glycerine, U.S.P. Standard, 2 cups; or urea crystals, 1 cup, when trough is used
- Working surface, with the seat of the chair at a convenient working height. The weaver may sit on a low stool with the chair held in front or fastened to a rigid revolving support, such as a piano stool
- Trough, table, or floor space to hold the rush and tools.
- Cutting tools: keyhole saw, knife, or shears to cut away the old seat and cut the ends of rush, a razor blade to trim loose ends of rush after the seat is finished
- Pliers to remove old nails or tacks and to cut wire
- Wood file to smooth rough places on the rails and to round the edges
- Clothes wringer to remove air and excess moisture from the rush
- Metal tool, such as a file with its surface smoothed, to remove air from the rush and to smooth the seat after it is woven. A dull case knife or putty knife may be substituted
- Carpenter's square and cardboard to measure seat and square rows
- Twine, such as green cotton fish line, strong enough to hold the ends of rush when weaving is started

- Clamp clothespins, about 6, to hold the twists of rush
- Block of soft wood, about 1" × 2" × 2", shaped to fit over the rails, to push the rows together
- Tack hammer
- Stuffer to poke the padding and to roll the seat. A ruler with wooden edge and a rolling pin may be substituted
- Cheesecloth to dampen and cover the seat
- Wire that bends easily, to hook the twists of rush through the small center opening when weaving is nearly finished
- Materials to finish the seat and a brush to apply them

PREPARE TO WEAVE

Remove the old seat and all old tacks or nails from the rails. Smooth any uneven places in the wood and round the edges if they are sharp and likely to break the rush.

Dampen the rush

Dampen the rush until it is workable enough to twist and weave without cracking or breaking. This may take 1 hour in warm water in a trough, or 8 to 12 hours spread on the floor and sprinkled.

Fill the trough about ¾ full of warm water. Add glycerine or urea crystals (about ¼ cup to 1 gallon of water) until the water feels soft. Soak the rush, a handful at a time, in the solution. Urea and glycerine help prevent the rush from drying out, but the solution may have to be changed during weaving, and both are expensive in the quantity needed.

Without a trough, you probably would dampen rush with warm water only.

Choose and prepare leaves

Choose long, unbroken leaves of about the same length, width, and thickness. The number of leaves to use in each strand depends not only on the leaves but on the size of strand you want. Usually, two leaves are twisted together; sometimes, if they are narrow or thin, three may be used. A thin strand is best for a graceful, delicate chair but many strands are needed to fill the seat. It is important to decide what size strands will look best on your chair.

Select and prepare the leaves and make them into strands as you work.

Run the leaves through a wringer to take out air from the cells and to make the leaves workable. Set the rollers tight so that the leaves make a sharp crackling noise as they are run through.

Draw each leaf quickly over the edge of the metal tool (Figure 2-16, page 18), to take out any air left in the cells. Continue the process while you are weaving.

Practice making twists

Cut off about 1 yard of cord, and loop it around the back-seat rail. Tie the ends of cord in a square knot (Figure 2-2); keep the loop about 5 inches long. (Note that ropes A and B are on the same side of rope C.) Arrange two leaves with a butt end and a tip end together and the flat side of one next to the rounded side of the other, like stacked spoons. Put one end of the pair about 3 inches through the loop of cord. Fold it toward the front rail and tie the ends of string around the bunch, making a square knot near the fold of rush (Figure 2-3). Tie the string temporarily around the side rail. Twist the leaves together, away from you and in such a way that the strand is smooth, even, and tight. Usually the thumb and first two fingers of one hand are used to make the twist, and the thumb and fingers of the other hand hold it. Keep the separate leaves straight and smooth as when making a braid; make long but firm twists, keeping the thumbs about 2 inches apart to assure a uniform twist (Figures 2-3 and 2-4). Practice until you make a smooth, even strand which is of a size and color that complements your chair. Untie the string around the side rail and take out this practice strand before starting to weave.

HOW TO WEAVE

The weaving of a firm smooth seat takes skill and practice. One satisfactory method is described in the following paragraphs.

Seats without corner blocks

With a carpenter's square as a guide, make a square of stiff cardboard, with the long side about 15 inches (Figure 2-5). Use this to mark off a square center

Figure 2-2

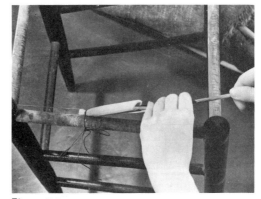

Figure 2-3

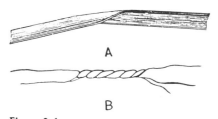

Figure 2-4

Figure 2-5

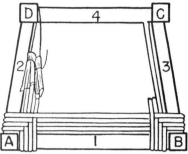

Figure 2-6

Figure 2-7

Figure 2-8

Figure 2-9

opening. Place the short side of the cardboard square parallel to either the front or the back rail and the long side against the inner edge of the corner of the back rail. Mark with a pencil on the front rail the outer edge of the square. Do the same on the other side of the seat. Adjust, if necessary, to make the distance between pencil lines on the front rail the same as between posts on the back rail.

Weave the corners first until you reach the marks on the front rail (Figure 2-6) and then weave as for a square seat (Figure 2-12, page 17). To do this:

Face the front of the chair, push the loop of string that was used for the practice twist close to the back post on the left side of the seat.

Begin with 4 leaves, each long enough to reach around three sides of the seat. Make two pairs, each with a butt and tip end together and the flat side of one leaf next to the round side of the other. Place one end of the pairs through the loop of cord about 3 inches. Fold them toward the front rail and use the ends of string to tie the bunch, making a square knot near the fold of rush.

Choose one pair of leaves, bring them almost to the front rail and then twist them into a strand. Turn this twist away from the post; keep all other twists in the same direction like a rope. Draw the strand over rail 1, close to post A, up through the opening of the chair, over the side rail 2, again close to the corner post A, and up through the opening again, thus holding the beginning of the twist (Figure 2-12). Lift the strand from the underside of the seat to shorten it, helping to make the seat firm (Figure 2-7). Lay the strands in position to make a square crossing and a seam straight from the corner of the seat.

Pull the strand, without twisting the leaves, across the front of the seat. At post B (Figure 2-12), twist the leaves, bring the strand over side rail 3, close to post B, up through the opening of the seat, over front rail 1, again close to post B. Arrange the strands as at post A.

Pull the strand, without twisting, to the back and fasten it firmly by winding the ends around the back rail and tying them together or by holding them with a clamp clothespin (Figure 2-8).

Strands are twisted only over the rails where they will show, not on the underside of the seat.

Weave the second pair in the same way. Loop the ends tightly around the back rail and fasten them with a clothespin to the first.

Tie more leaves, one pair at a time, in the same loop of string and weave in the same way. About 5 twists fill 1 inch. Use a piece of rush or the cardboard square every 2 or 3 rows to make sure that the corners are square and the rows straight (Figure 2-9). Use the hammer and block of wood to force the strands in place (Figure 2-10). Keep the seam straight from the corner toward the center of the seat. Make a square crossing; add from 4 to 6 inches of another leaf to fill out a thin strand (Figure 2-14, page 18).

After the corners are woven as far as the marks on the front rail (Figure 2-8), fasten the ends on the right-hand side: tie with a square knot a piece of string about 18 inches long around all the ends of rush. Loop the ends of string around the back rail and tie another knot. Pull the strands taut and keep the rows straight and close together. Remove the clothespins and cut away the rush over the rail (Figure 2-11, underside of chair).

If the rush breaks, replace it with another piece.

Padding. After the front corners are filled in, pad them. The padding is put in the pockets on the underside of the seat at each side of the corner seams. Butt ends and short lengths of rush are folded the length of the opening and forced in flat bunches from the center toward the corner posts. To do this, turn the chair over. Use the wooden stuffer (Figure 2-1) and poke a bunch of rush into the pocket on the underside of the seat, from the center to the seam (Figure 2-11). The finished seat should be hard and flat, or slightly rounded, but not overstuffed. Rush shrinks as it dries, so put in enough padding to make the seat firm but not fat. Both front corners should be of the same thickness.

As you continue to weave around all four corners, add padding about every 3 inches. Back corners take less padding than do front corners. When you have finished the weaving, add the last padding by poking in bunches parallel to the last strands.

Square seats

Seat frames may be square or have corner blocks that make the opening square (Figure 2-23, page 19). Weave these seats, and seats that are wider at the front, after you have filled the corners as follows:

Weaving the first strand, corner A (Figure 2-12). Use the same loop that you had for seats wider at the front or make a similar loop if you are just starting to weave a square seat. Tie in the butt ends of two leaves, one of which is long, and the other short. Twist and weave around post A (Figure 2-12).

Loops of string seldom have to be cut; weaving covers them.

Joining the rush. As you leave corner A (Figures 2-12 and 2-13), add a new leaf. Place this between the weaving and the strand, with the butt end hanging down below the underside of the seat about 6 inches, or the amount of the stiff end of the leaf, with the curved side toward you (Figure 2-13). Twist this new leaf with the other two about twice to hold them together. The butt ends make a seam on the underside of the seat and should hang down rather than be caught in the weaving. Always add a new piece of rush after you finish each corner so when weaving the next corner the rush will be securely fastened and you will have enough to go around that corner.

Adding rush. Occasionally you may need to use a third piece of rush to fill out the strand, as when crossing twists at the seam (Figure 2-14).

Continuing the first strand. Continue to corner B (Figure 2-12). If the strand is too "fat," drop the end of the shortest leaf. This can be cut off or folded in for padding. Twist and weave around corner B. As you leave this corner, again add a new leaf. Continue to corner C and weave. Add a new piece of rush, proceed to and weave around corner D, again adding a piece of rush (Figure 2-12).

Figure 2-10

Figure 2-11

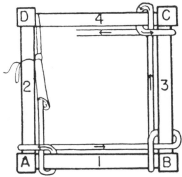
Figure 2-12

Figure 2-13

Figure 2-14

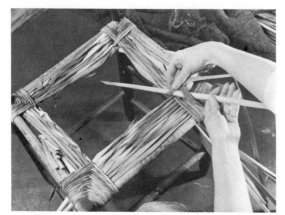

Figure 2-15

Figure 2-16

Figure 2-17

Figure 2-18

Splicing. If rush breaks or you do not have enough to finish weaving the corner, another piece may be spliced in (Figure 2-15). After you weave the first half of the corner, add a new leaf at the seam with the butt end extending about 6 inches below the seat. Twist the old leaves once around the new to lock it. Then arrange the leaves parallel and twist all three together. If the strand is too thick, pull out the shortest leaf. Continue, weaving the second half of the corner. On the underside of the chair these butt ends will stick down, but at an opposite angle from those used for joining, and will be cut off.

Weaving the rest of the seat. Go on weaving, as for the first strand, around post A to posts B, C, and D, (Figure 2-12) until there is only space for two more rows on the side rails. Continue to make the rush workable by running it through the wringer and using the metal tool (Figure 2-16). Smooth the twists (Figure 2-17). Join a new piece of rush after each corner. Pad the seat as you weave (Figure 2-18). Keep the strands taut, rows straight, by pounding them with the block of wood, seams straight and the opposite sides of the chair alike (Figure 2-16). Check as you go along to see that the opposite openings measure the same and that you have the same number of twists over each rail. Occasionally force the metal tool quickly between the rows to straighten them and to smooth the strands. Before the rush dries out, roll and polish the strands with the round end of the stuffer until the seat is smooth (Figure 2-25, page 20).

If the sides are shorter than the back, fill the sides and then weave from back to front in a figure 8: To help prevent holes near the center, weave around the right side rail twice for the last two strands, proceed to the left rail (Figure 2-19) and weave around it twice. Then weave in a figure 8 over back and front rails until those rails are filled in (Figure 2-20). Sometimes this process

Figure 2-19

Figure 2-20

Figure 2-21

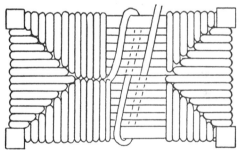

Figure 2-22

is reversed. Join the rush at the center after weaving the front rail, or after weaving around both rails.

Pull the last few strands through the small opening with a hook made of wire (Figure 2-1). Weave in as many rows as possible; when you think the seat is filled, add one more strand. Fasten the last strand on the underside of the chair by separating the ends, winding each one around a nearby strand (Figure 2-21), and tying them firmly with a square knot.

If the unfinished seat is left overnight, fasten the last twist to the seat with a clamp clothespin. Cover the seat with wet cheesecloth, to keep the rush from drying out.

Seats wider than deep

Weave until the sides are filled as directed for a square seat. See that the opening measures the same on one side as the other, and the front the same as the back. Complete the filling of the back and front rails by weaving twists in a figure 8, going over and under the front rail, up through the opening, over and under the back rail, and again up through the opening. If you finish weaving the corners on the left-hand side of the seat, weave from there in a figure 8 until the opening is completely filled (Figure 2-22). You may reverse this, weaving from the right side or the back rail first.

Just before making the figure 8, you may weave twice around side rail, instead of the single strands as shown in Figure 2-22.

Seats with corner blocks

The chair in Figure 2-23 has corner blocks which substitute for filling corners. Weave around four sides, beginning at the back left corner.

Figure 2-23

Figure 2-24

Figure 2-25

Figure 2-26

HOW TO FINISH THE SEAT*

After you have completed the weaving and padding, trim the butt ends on the lower side of the seat to about 1 inch, so that they do not show as you face the chair (Figure 2-24). Trim any loose ends with a razor blade or shears. Use the rounded end of the stuffer to pound and even the seat.

On the upper side, trim the loose ends, straighten the rows, and pound with the stuffer to mold and polish the twists (Figure 2-25). You may use a piece of leather also for polishing.

Let the trimmed and polished seat (Figure 2-26) dry thoroughly. Depending on drying conditions this may take from one to four weeks.

When dry, to help prevent the rush from becoming brittle and breaking, apply at least two coats of one of the following penetrating or resilient coatings to both sides of the seat:

½ gum turpentine and ½ linseed oil. Apply two coats, one day apart.

Penetrating wood sealer (tung oil and varnish resins). Two coats one day apart. Apply, let stand for 20 minutes, wipe off excess.

Oil-modified polyurethane. (Contains mineral spirits, or its solvent is mineral spirits.) Two coats one day apart. Apply, let stand for 20 minutes, wipe off excess.

As wear becomes evident apply additional coats. Be sure no one sits in the chair until the finish has dried thoroughly.

*Revised by Clark Garner, Assoc. Prof., Dept. Design and Environmental Analysis, New York State College of Human Ecology, Cornell University, Ithaca, N.Y.

Fiber Rush Seats

Fiber rush is made from a very tough grade of paper twisted into a strand to resemble rush. It may be purchased in dark brown in widths 3/32 inch, 4/32 inch, 5/32 inch, and 6/32 inch to resemble antique rush seats, and in multicolored strands in 6/32 inch to resemble new seats.

EQUIPMENT YOU NEED

- Chair—same type as for real rush
- Fiber rush, 2–3 pounds; 4/32 or 5/32 inch width. (6/32 inch is coarser and used mostly for large seats and porch furniture.)
- Working surface, table, cutting tools, pliers, wood file, metal tool, carpenter's square, clamp clothespins, block of soft wood, hammer, stuffer, and wire (see page 14)
- Twine, such as cotton fish line, about 10 yards
- Fine wire, all-purpose glue, or transparent fish line to fasten ends of rush
- Padding—corrugated boxes, the equivalent of 8 flat pieces, each 10 inches by 18 inches

PREPARE TO WEAVE

Prepare the chair, (see page 14). Buy the fiber in pound or 2-pound lots, or in quantity on a large reel. Pound lots cost a few cents more; reels take time to unroll and rewind. On a reel, roll and unroll the rush rather than pull it. Take off about 25 yards to work with at one time. Tie the end to a nearby strand, and wind it in a roll about 6 inches across. Twenty-five yards of 5/32-inch width fiber weighs about one-half pound. Tie string in a slip knot around the roll so that it won't unwind or untwist.

HOW TO WEAVE

Use one strand and weave as you do real rush. The fiber is already twisted. Dampen the fiber by dipping the roll in and out of warm water; if wet, the paper softens and cannot be used.

For seats wide at the front, cut separate lengths each time you weave around the two front corners. For square or oblong openings, use one long strand.

To begin weaving, fasten the ends of the fiber as for real rush, but alternate hooking and tying ends to a nearby strand to make them less bulky. Each time you weave the corners, tighten the preceding strand.

Join the fiber by one of three methods: (1) fold back the ends of fiber and wire them together; or (2) overlap the ends about 3 inches and tie them together with very fine wire, fish line, or heavy thread; or (3) tie the end with a square knot on the underside of the seat.

Padding. If firmly woven, and seat rails are about the same height, padding may be omitted. To tighten loose strands, add heavy corrugated cardboard. Other cardboard or heavy paper can be used but may rustle. Begin padding after four or five inches are woven on the front rail. If the rails are of even height, cut four pieces of cardboard, one to fit each section of the seat. Force them under the weaving from the upper side of the seat. If rails are of uneven height, two pieces of cardboard may be used in each section. More padding may be added. A hole about 2 inches square must be left in the cardboard at the center of the seat to get the fiber through. If brown paper is used, cut it in squares and fold it in triangles.

To fasten the end of fiber, after weaving is completed, pull it to the underside of the seat, untwist the paper, cut it in half, wind each around a nearby strand, and tie.

Unfasten joinings which are conspicuous, overlap the ends, and glue or wire them together.

Seats should be finished as for natural rush.

3. HONG KONG GRASS, ROPE AND TWINE SEATS

You can weave attractive, inexpensive chair seats with Hong Kong grass, rope, or twine. In a few hours, with simple equipment, a discarded piece of furniture can be brought back to use.

SELECT THE CHAIR

Select a chair which is sturdy and simple in line and design. Seat rails must be round, or deep and flat, so that you can wind around them. If rails are about the same length, and straight rather than noticeably curved, strands of grass and rope stay in place. Strands slip if side rails slant so that the front rail is more than 3 inches wider than the back. For such chairs, filling in corners, as with rush seats, rather than weaving in a design may be preferable.

SELECT THE WEAVING MATERIAL

Choose one of several materials to weave the seat:

Hong Kong grass is hand twisted, and looks like rope except strands vary slightly in width. Grass seats have interesting texture and can be woven on round rails, in a variety of designs. Grass is not as smooth to weave or sit on as natural or fiber rush.

You can buy Hong Kong grass at chair seating and crafts-supply houses and from mail-order firms.

Rope is smooth, firmly twisted, and does not stretch. Use off-white sisal or hemp (preferably 4-ply), 4-thread manila trawl twine, nylon yacht cord, venetian blind cord (about size 6), or sash cord (about size 4). All of these can be woven on round seat rails.

You can buy these materials at rope and cordage supply houses, marine supply houses, hardware stores, and lumberyards.

Plastic clothesline is one of the least expensive and easiest materials to use. Choose the kind with a wire center so it will not stretch easily; use on round seat rails only.

Wool tie twine is an inexpensive twisted paper similar to fiber rush, which can be used on chairs with wide seat rails. Such rails support the twine and help make the seat strong.

PREPARE THE CHAIR

Bevel rails with a wood rasp or coarse sandpaper so rough or sharp edges will not cut the weaving material.

Remodel and reglue the chair, if necessary. If the old finish is worn, remove it and refinish or paint the chair. Be sure the finish is thoroughly dry before you start to weave the seat.

Place masking tape around the posts to protect the finish while you weave.

Hong Kong Grass

Heddle

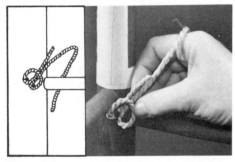

Figure 3-1

Figure 3-2

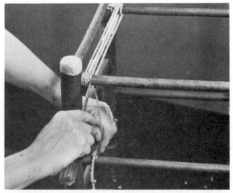

Figure 3-3

EQUIPMENT YOU NEED

- Hong Kong grass, about 2 pounds for a seat 14 inches across the front, sold in coils of about 3 pounds
- Upholsterer's tacks, No. 8; 4 per chair
- Tack hammer
- Shears
- Heddle, a weaving aid which holds the grass. It is made of corrugated paper, about 12 inches long and 6 inches wide, cut the long way of the corrugation; or, piece of shingle, same size as above, optional
- Soft string to tie the hank, about 1 yard
- Strong thread, such as carpet thread, about 1 yard
- Pencil
- Ruler or steel rule
- Tongue depressors, about 18, or 2 thin, narrow pliable sticks, like yardsticks, each about 18 inches long, to use in planning the design
- Screwdriver, block or stick of soft wood, meat skewer, or similar strong tool to push strands together

MARKING THE CHAIR

Measure between front posts, and with a pencil mark the center of the front rail and the center of the back rail.

PREPARE THE GRASS

Make a heddle of the corrugated paper, as shown in drawing. Cut a slit (A) to hold the end of grass. Tape the corners so they will not break. Or, make a loop of about 40 yards of grass, as shown in Figure 3-6, page 25.

To make the grass pliable enough to weave, moisten it by sprinkling it with warm water or by dipping the heddle in a pan of warm water until all the grass is wet but the cardboard is still firm.

Grass is wrapped around the rails from back to front and woven side to side, making a double seat.

WARPING
(wrapping grass around back and front rails)

Work from left to right, as you face the chair.

Fasten the end of grass to the back rail, near the left post as follows:

Drive 2 tacks part way in on the inside of the rail, as near the bottom as possible and with just enough space for only 2 strands of grass between the nails.

Make a loop about 6 inches long and place the two parallel ends between the tacks.

Bring the loop toward the ends and around the outside of the tacks (Figure 3-1).

Pull the ends to tighten the fastening and pound the tacks to hold it securely.

Wind the strand over and under the back rail. Bring it across the underside of the seat, under the front rail, and then wind around the rail. Pull the strand taut but be careful not to break or weaken it (Figure 3-2). Bring the strand over the rail and across the top of the seat, then over and under the back rail. Continue the strand on the underside of the seat to the front, wind under and over the rail. Then wind under and over the same rail again and bring the strand to the back rail, winding over and under that rail. This completes one repeat.

Because the front is wider than the back, the front is filled by winding around the rail between *each* cross strand. At the back, rails will be wound between *two* cross strands, rather than between each strand.

After each repeat (between **), pull carefully to tighten the grass. Use a screw driver or other firm tool to force strands close together. Keep the weaving flat, however. Figure 3-3 shows one repeat, and starting the next.

Continue wrapping, beginning the next repeat at the *. If strands begin to wear or break, wrap them in masking tape (Figure 3-4). Remove this later, if it shows.

At the center of the seat, strands should be straight from back to front (Figure 3-5). They may be apart slightly on the back rail but forced together on the front rail.

When the opening becomes too small to force the heddle through, wind the grass over your arm and hand to make a long loop, as you wind yarn. Leave a yard or more of the strand to work with and tie string around the rest of the loop and the end so the grass will tangle less.

Wrap the right front corner as you did the left, that is, under and over the rail. To get ready to weave side to side, pull this strand under and then over the right side rail. Fasten temporarily with a clamp clothespin (Figure 3-6).

WEAVING
(from side rail to side rail)

Use tongue depressors or 2 thin pliable sticks to plan the design. Count the number of warp strands; this chair, which is 13½ inches between front posts and 11 inches between back posts, has 40. Plan a pattern to fit the chair; use an even number of strands, rather than an odd number, if possible. For example, weaving might be in units of 4, using pairs of warp strands together at the front rail (Figure 3-7).

A larger mesh can be used for a larger seat. The chair in Figure 3-8 has 48 strands. A suggested design is: 4-11-3-12-3-11-4 (total 48). This design is the same on the two sides and also each side of center, but pairs are divided so the design is more difficult to follow. Also strands in such an open mesh may catch or pull as the seat is used (see also Figure 3-18, page 27).

The pattern chosen for the seat illustrated, which has 40 warp strands in units of 4 (over 4, under 4), is

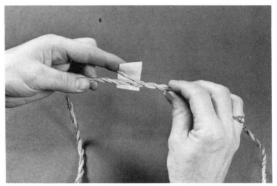

Figure 3-4

Figure 3-5

Figure 3-6

Figure 3-7

Hong Kong Grass, Rope and Twine Seats **25**

Figure 3-8

Figure 3-9

Figure 3-10

Figure 3-11

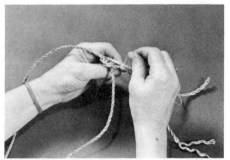

Figure 3-12

Figure 3-13

Figure 3-14

easy to weave. Release the clothespin and enough grass to weave across. Using only the warp strands on top of the seat, weave across from side to side and hold the strand over the side rail. Bring this strand to the front as far as the posts allow (Figure 3-9).

Turn the chair over and weave from side to side using only the strands on the underside of the seat. Follow the same design; that is, weave under and over the same strands as you did on the top. Since you wove under the 4 strands as you finished the left end of the row on top, weave under those strands as you start across on the bottom of the seat (Figure 3-10), weaving under 4, over 4, across the row, and again over the rail. Continue in the same way until you have 4 strands across the top of the seat, finishing on the left side rail. (On this chair, 11 units of 4 strands fill side rails. This number would vary as the length of rails varies.) Wind twice around that rail. Turn the chair over and weave across the bottom to complete the fourth row underneath. Turn the chair right side up and wind twice around the right side rail and bring the strand to the top.

For the next 4 filler strands, reverse the design, first under 4, then over 4, etc. Winding twice around rails between each group of 4 fillers helps to keep cross rows straight.

When you need more grass, prepare enough to finish weaving the seat. Tie the ends together, with a square knot, on the underside of the seat (Figure 3-11). Hold the ends by wrapping with strong thread (Figure 3-12).

Continue weaving, pushing strands together on the rails (Figure 3-13). When you reach the back posts, the design is complete (Figure 3-14).

Figure 3-15

Figure 3-16

Figure 3-17

Figure 3-18

Figure 3-19

To end weaving, weave across the underside (Figure 3-15). Allowing about 4 inches, cut the strand, and tuck the end in the pocket between the top and bottom of the seat. With strong thread tie square knots to secure this strand to nearby warp strands (Figure 3-16). The fastening is inconspicuous. The completed chair is shown in Figure 3-17.

OTHER DESIGNS

In the chair shown in Figure 3-18, warping is the same as for the previous chair. The weaving design is: 4-9-3-10-3-9-4. For this seat only the warps on top are used in weaving; the underside is not woven (Figure 3-19). This method is quicker but somewhat less sturdy than weaving both sides.

A variety of other designs can be chosen. The most satisfactory are balanced on each half of the seat, with the mesh close enough so strands will not pull or catch as you use the chair.

Hong Kong grass also may be woven like rope. See page 31.

Rope

Figure 3-20

Figure 3-21

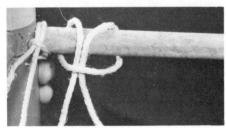

Figure 3-22

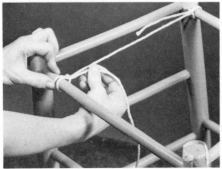

Figure 3-23

EQUIPMENT YOU NEED

• Rope or twine, usually available in 5 lb. balls; about 1½ lb. for a chair 16 inches across the front, 2 lbs. for a larger chair
• Staple gun with 5/16-inch staples. You probably can rent or borrow a staple gun from a lumberyard or a store which does upholstery work; or, one dozen upholstery tacks, No. 8, and tack hammer
• Pliers, long-nose
• Glue—a white glue that dries clear } for ends of rope
• Masking tape
• Cardboard, about 18 inches long and 6 inches wide
• Awl
• Other supplies as listed for Hong Kong grass, except only 2 or 3 tongue depressors are needed

PREPARE THE CHAIR

Square the center opening: using a carpenter's square, cut a cardboard pattern of a size that will fit within the chair rails. Fit this close against back posts, parallel with the back rail. A cardboard, such as the back of a tablet, helps to support the square (Figure 3-20). Make two marks on the front rail corresponding to the length between the back rails. Distances from the marks to the front corner posts may not be the same on each side of the chair, if side rails slant at different angles. Place masking tape around the posts, near the rails, to protect the finish.

PREPARE THE ROPE

Pull the end of rope from the inside of the ball. Measure and cut off about 40 yards, winding it on a heddle as in Figure 3-2. Or wind it over your hand and arm in a hank about 12 inches long, as you would wind yarn. Leave about 1 yard to work with and tie the hank with string.

Fasten the end to the inside of the left side rail with a staple gun. Fasten in 2 or 3 places (Figure 3-21). Or use 2 tacks, as for Hong Kong grass.

WARPING
(wrapping rope around back and front rails)

Strands are knotted each time around the rails.

From the side fastening, bring the cord over and under the back rail, up in the seat to the left of the cord over the rail. Cross over this cord, holding the crossing with your left hand. Weave under and over the back rail and bring the heddle down through the loop. Draw the knot tight. All knots are inside the seat opening, ends of rope are parallel and under the cross strands. For each knot, two cords are wound around the rail. Figure 3-22

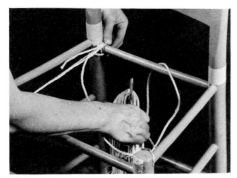

Figure 3-24

Figure 3-25

shows the detail of the knot, and Figure 3-23 shows the knot drawn tight on the back rail.

Bring the strand from the back to the mark on the front rail, holding it firmly but not tightly. Corners are filled in later. Knot around the front rail (Figure 3-23). Knot again at the back (Figure 3-24).

Continue around each rail until the center square is filled. The back rail should be covered. Knots should be snug, but not tight. If forced together too tightly they will bunch rather than lie smoothly. If strands are drawn tight, weaving will be difficult and the seat hard to sit on. End at the back rail, at the right corner post.

WEAVING
(from side rail to side rail)

Weaving is done from side to side, from the back toward the front, and only on the top of the seat.

Continue with the same warp strand. Bring this in front of the post, over the rail, and knot as before (Figure 3-25).

Then plan the design. Diagonal or square patterns can be used, depending on the design of the chair. Block or square designs are suitable for seat openings that are nearly square. Diagonal patterns can be used either on square openings or those wider across the front. Work with strands that are paired at the front; weaving then is easier. The simplest designs are woven over and under the same number of strands, as few as 6 strands (3 pairs) or as many as 18 strands (9 pairs). With less than 3 pairs, cross strands are difficult to force in place; a mesh larger than 9 pairs has long strands which might catch and pull as the chair is used.

The second row determines the pattern. For diagonal motifs, weave one pair to the left (or right) each row; for square designs, reverse each row.

Count the knots on the front rail; the chair illustrated had 30 knots. Use a pliable stick or tongue depressors and try out several possible weaves. In Figure 3-26, the weave would be over 6 strands (3 pairs) and under 6 strands (3 pairs). If a mesh of over 4 and under 4 were used, 3 strands would be left to weave at each side of the seat (Figure 3-27).

A mesh of over and under 3 was first tried for this chair. From the right side rail, weave across to the left

Figure 3-26

Figure 3-27

Figure 3-28

Figure 3-29

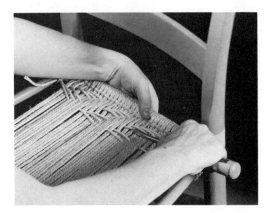

Figure 3-30

Figure 3-31

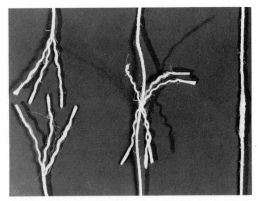

Figure 3-32

Figure 3-33

and make a knot on that rail. Use one stick as a heddle and a second thinner stick to push the strand as near the back rail as possible (Figure 3-28).

Weave back, on top of the seat. To start a diagonal design, count the warp strands from near the center of the opening and weave one pair to the left (or right). The design cannot always be complete at side rails (Figure 3-29).

After weaving 3 or 4 rows, if the mesh is too fine to force the rows together, take it out and try a larger one. In Figure 3-30 weaving is changed to over 4 pairs and under 4 pairs. After 5 or 6 rows are woven, they should hold the first rows in place. After this as you weave each row, push the previous row in place.

When you need more rope, tie ends together in a square knot on the underside of the seat (Figure 3-31). On the right side the end has been tied to the strand with heavy thread and covered with glue to prevent fraying. The left end, which was protected with masking tape during weaving, will be trimmed and fastened also. Or, if rope is 3-ply, splice ends as in Figure 3-32).

WARPING CORNERS

Separate strands, one on each side, are used to fill corners. Cut lengths, allowing about 1 yard for each knot around the front rail; for this chair, 3 yards for 3 knots.

If side rails are nearly straight, these corner strands can be fastened to each side rail after you have woven 6 or 8 knots. Strands can be wrapped temporarily around the front rail.

If side rails slant noticeably, continue side to side weaving to the front rail. Follow the pattern from near the center, rather than counting at the sides, and keep together the pairs of strands over the front rail.

Fasten the end on the underside by looping through or tying to a nearby strand. Use strong thread to tie the strands. Glue the end to prevent fraying (Figure 3-33).

To complete a corner, insert one of the separate strands as far back as there is space for it. In Figure 3-34 the end of the strand was pushed to the underside, in front of the back post. This warp strand is woven to complete the diagonal design, in this case over 4 and under 4. A screwdriver or similar blunt tool is used to force the strands apart. Continue weaving toward the front (Figure 3-35). Knot on front rail and weave back, pairing this strand with the one before.

Figure 3-34

Figure 3-35

Figure 3-36

Figure 3-37

Figure 3-38

Weave toward the back, as far as there is space for the strand (plan to match the design, also)—for this chair, the second diagonal band from the back corner. Bring the strand over a cross strand, to the underside of the chair, then bring it up to the right side to continue the design. Weave to the front and knot there; weave back pairing the strands. Make a third knot in a similar way (usually there will be space for no more than 5 knots) and weave as far as you can to complete the design (Figure 3-37).

Weave the second corner, continuing the design on that side of the seat.

Fasten the ends of the underside of the seat by knotting or looping to a nearby strand. Tie with strong thread wherever necessary to secure the fastening; glue the ends to prevent fraying (Figure 3-36). Figure 3-37 shows the finished seat.

HONG KONG GRASS WOVEN LIKE ROPE

In this method of weaving, knots are less firm and grass pulls apart more than in winding as on page 24.

Figure 3-38 shows a finished seat. The top one of the pair of warp strands is used in weaving diagonally side to side. The other is not woven and forms the under-part of the seat (see Figure 3-19, page 27).

Wool Tie Twine

Figure 3-39

Figure 3-42

Figure 3-40

Figure 3-41

Chairs with deep seat rails can have seats and backs woven of wool tie twine. Two balls of twine are needed for each.

The old oak dining room chair in Figure 3-40 had a slip seat and knobs on the front posts. The wood was given a blond finish.

Mark the center opening, as in Figure 3-20, page 28.

Fasten the cord as in Figure 3-1, page 24.

Wrap around rails, keeping the twine straight from back to front. Leave strands slack rather than taut so that weaving will be easier. For the corners, cut two continuous pieces as in weaving rope, page 29. Fasten each to the inside of a side rail, near the back. Bring to the front, wind around the rail temporarily, and leave the bunch until side to side weaving is finished.

Weave side to side; the design in Figure 3-39 is in squares of 7. Weave the corners to complete the design. Tack to hold ends, on the inside of the rail. The completed chair is shown in Figure 3-40.

The underside is woven like the top. Tie square knots to join ends of twine (Figure 3-41).

The back can be woven like the seat (Figure 3-42).

Plastic Clothesline

Figure 3-43

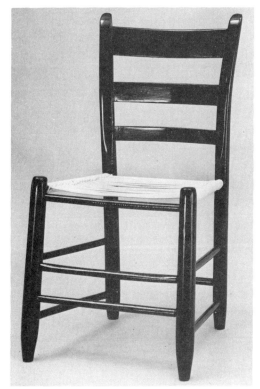

Figure 3-44

Paint the chair a dark color to accent the white clothesline. The completed chair is shown in Figure 3-44.

Use a small chair (no wider than 14 inches across the front) and buy 100 feet of clothesline. Wind on a heddle (see page 24). Since there is no feasible way to join clothesline, the strands are wrapped side to side only, and knotted around side rails (Figure 3-43).

How to Finish the Seats

Seats of Hong Kong grass, smooth rope, and plastic clothesline need no finish to protect them. Apply a clear furniture sealer or shellac to rope seats, if they feel scratchy, and to seats of wool tie twine so they will roughen and soil less quickly. Two or three thin coats usually are desirable; apply on the underside as well as the top. Be sure each coat is thoroughly dry before you apply the next or before you use the chair.

All of these seats can be cleaned with water or with mild soap suds. Use a damp cloth or a soft brush; avoid using so much water that you soften the weaving material. Rinse and dry quickly and thoroughly, preferably out of doors in a breeze.

4. SPLINT SEATS

SELECT THE CHAIR

Splint chair seats are made of wood that has been cut in long thin strips and interwoven in various patterns. The chair on which splint can be used must have seat rails so that you can wind the splint around them. Such chairs also may have seats of splint-type materials (reed or wide binding cane) or of rush; the original seat, if you have it, usually indicates which to use.

Splint is suitable for chairs simple in design, with few turnings, such as the Early American ladder-back chairs. Often it is used when side rails are higher than front and back rails. If side rails slant so the front of the seat is more than 3 inches wider than the back, choose rush or a material no wider than ⅜ inch so the strands will stay in place without slipping on the side rails.

Splint and flat reed are used for indoor furniture, while flat oval reed and wide binding cane are used for outdoor furniture.

SELECT THE SPLINT

Splint is obtained from native ash and from the tropical rattan palm. Native splint should be cut from select straight grain second-growth timber and machine cut to a uniform width.

The tropical palm from which materials like splint are made grows in the Indonesian Archipelago, China,

India, Ceylon, and the Malay Peninsula. Without its leaves it is known commercially as *rattan*. The outer bark, stripped in different widths, is sold as *cane;* the core, split into round and flat strips of different thicknesses and widths, is called *reed*.

These materials are available from dealers of seat-weaving supplies, mail-order houses, and local stores. They are all sold either in bunches containing enough for one chair or in quantity lots. Costs per seat are about the same. Real splint makes a better looking seat than does flat reed, but reed may be easier for beginners to weave.

Widths of splint vary:

Splint	1/2 inch, 5/8 inch, and 3/4 inch Buy 1 pound of 5/8-inch width for seat of average size (16 inches across front)
Flat reed	1/4 inch, 3/8 inch, and 1/2 inch Buy 1 pound of 3/8-inch width for 16-inch seat
Flat oval reed	3/16 inch and 3/8 inch Buy 1 pound for 16-inch seat; 1-1/2 pound for 18-inch or larger seat
Wide binding cane	About 3/16 inch Buy 1 bunch of 500 feet for 18-inch seat

Figure 4-1—Equipment.

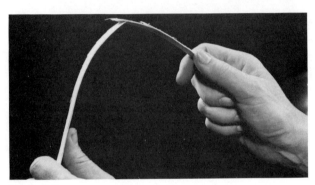

Figure 4-2

The width you need depends on the style and size of chair and on the place the chair is to be used. Narrower widths take longer to weave than wider ones, but wider ones may look heavy or bulky.

Fiber (paper) splint is not shown in this book; it is less durable than other kinds of splint.

EQUIPMENT YOU NEED

- 1. Splint of the desired type and width
- 2. Shears
- 3. Keyhole saw
- 4. Pan, oval, about 14 by 18 inches for splint and reed
  Bowl about 11 inches in diameter for flat oval reed
  Bowl about 6 inches in diameter for wide binding cane
- 5. Glycerine, U.S.P. Standard
  For splint, reed—1 cup glycerine to 10 cups water
  For flat oval reed—1/2 cup glycerine to 5 cups water
  For wide binding cane—1/3 cup glycerine to 4 cups water or
  Urea crystals, 4 tablespoons to 1 quart of water
- 6. Sponge, cloths, or towel

- 7. Cardboard from which to cut the shape of a carpenter's square, the long arm about 18 inches, the short end about 6 inches (see page 37)
- 8. Steel measure and sharp pencil
- 9. String to fasten the end of the strand
- 10. Clamp clothespins, 6
- 11. Staple gun/gun tacker and staples—1/4-inch size
- 12. Stick of soft wood—1-inch lumber, 1/4 inch thick and about 18 inches long
- 13. Pliers, long-nose
- 14. Screwdriver with blunt end or a similar tool to force the splint in place
- 15. Razor blade
- 16. Blending seat stain, if desired, and cloth to apply

PREPARE TO WEAVE

The seat

If old seating remains, cut it away, but save it as a guide. You may find padding between the layers, but shaped seats without stuffing usually are more comfortable to sit on. Pull out all nails and tacks and clean any dust from the seat rails. If you need to paint or refinish the wood, be sure it is done before you begin weaving.

The splint

Pull one of the pieces of splint from the looped end of the hank, near where it is tied. As you pull, shake the hank so the splint will not tangle or roughen. Bend the piece between your fingers. The right side is smooth; the wrong side splinters as in Figure 4-2. With the smooth or beveled side out, roll it to fit the pan or bowl in which it is to soak. Fasten the ends with a clamp clothespin. Prepare 3 or 4 pieces in the same way. Ash splint, 5/8 inch wide, is used for the chair illustrated.

Soak the splint in a solution of glycerine, or of urea crystals. Either helps to shape the splint. The crystals increase its strength; but glycerine is preferred because it helps to retain moisture and keep the splint from

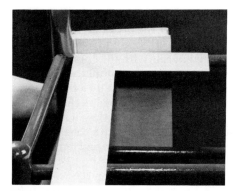

Figure 4-3

Figure 4-4

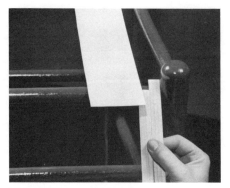

Figure 4-5

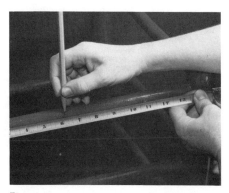

Figure 4-6

Figure 4-7

drying out and cracking. To hasten the soaking process, use warm water in the solution. Lay the roll in the appropriate container and let it soak until it is soft and pliable—about 1/2 hour for splint and about 20 minutes for flat reed, flat oval reed, and binding cane. Each time you remove a roll from the pan, put another one in to soak while you work.

HOW TO WEAVE

Weaving is done in two directions: the first, called *warping,* is the wrapping of the splint around the seat rails. Usually this is done from the back to the front of the chair, or the long way of the opening, so that the second step, called *weaving,* can be done across the open rails, from side to side or the short way of the opening. Both sides of the seat are woven so that they look alike when finished.

All splints woven one way on the top of the seat are at right angles to those woven the other way. If the front of the seat is wider than the back, weave the center first and fill in the corners later with short lengths.

Warping

Mark a center rectangle or square: using a carpenter's square, cut a cardboard pattern of a size that will fit within the chair rails. Fit this close against one back post, parallel with the back rail (Figure 4-3).

Mark the front corner of the square on the front rail (Figure 4-4). Repeat on the other side of the seat. Check to see that you have enough space for the width of splint. If the two sides vary, adjust by marking a slightly greater allowance on the shorter side and less on the long side (Figure 4-5).

Mark on the front rail the center between these two marks (Figure 4-6).

Mark the center on the back rail (Figure 4-7).

Take the roll of splint from the bowl in which it is soaking and remove the excess water with your fingers or a sponge or cloth. Put another piece in to soak while you work.

Work with the full length of the piece. Tie one end to the left side rail with string, with the right side of the splint next to the wood, so that you work with the grain

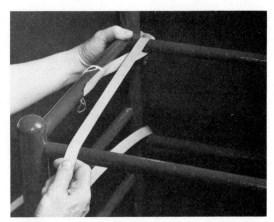

Figure 4-8

Figure 4-9

Figure 4-10

Figure 4-11

and the smooth side is outside. Pull the strand under, and then up and over the back rail, close to the post, in the exact position and shape you want it to dry. Pull the strand to the front rail, with the outside edge exactly at the pencil mark (Figure 4-8). Pull the strand over and under the rail and then return it to the back rail.

Continue until you have used all the piece. Force the wet strands close together so they will not slip on the rail; splint shrinks more in width than in length. Keep strands equally taut. Secure the end temporarily with a clamp clothespin (Figure 4-9).

Join pieces on the underside: place a new piece under the old, with the right side down. Lay a stick of soft wood across the rails, under the strands, and staple the strands together in three places, 1 to 2 inches apart, so that at least one of them can be covered when you weave the other way (Figure 4-10). Pull the strand away from the stick and with pliers flatten the ends of the staples (Figure 4-18, page 40). When legs of staples are down, they show less, but could scratch as you work. Staples which show can usually be removed or covered. Leave enough of the old strand to support the new, but cut off any that would make a double thickness around the rail. Pull the new strand under and around the rail (Figure 4-11).

Continue wrapping strands. When you reach the center mark, count the warp strands to make sure you will have the same number on each half of the seat. When you reach the pencil mark on the right side of the chair, use a clamp clothespin to hold the warp. If work is interrupted, sprinkle the seat and dampen the end to keep the splint pliable.

You may want to use the old seat as a guide in deciding the pattern of the weave. Or, you can use scraps and ends of splints to try out different designs. Or, work out designs on squared paper as illustrated in Figure 4-35, page 42.

Count the number of warp strands on the back rail. This number may be evenly divisible by the number in the design you want to use: for example, 20 strands and a pattern of 2 over and 2 under, or 21 strands with a pattern of 3 over and 3 under. If the number is not evenly divisible, you may use the same pattern if you:

1. Plan from near the center of the opening and begin weaving accordingly. For example: if there are 23 strands and a pattern of 3 over 3 under, weave over 1 to start the row, continue across until you have used 21 strands, and then weave the single strand as on the first side.
2. Plan to use a diagonal design. Emphasis then will be away from the side rails where the design may or may not be completed. A diagonal design also is desirable if side rails are uneven.

The second row determines how you use the design. You can move one or more strands to the left for a diagonal design from the right back to the left front of the seat, or you may reverse the direction. For a geometric design, weave alternate rows alike.

Weaving, which makes the design, frequently is:
   Over 2 and under 2

A close weave is difficult to achieve with patterns less than over 2 and under 2.

Figure 4-12

Figure 4-13

Figure 4-14

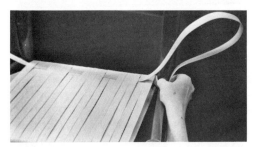

Figure 4-15

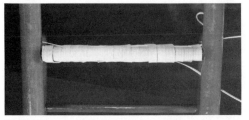

Figure 4-16

Figure 4-17

Other designs are:
    Over 2 and under 3
    Over 3 and under 3
    Large seats or narrow strands, 3/8 inch or less, may
be woven:
    Over 4 and under 4
    Over 4 and under 2
    Over 5 and under 3

The above combinations may be reversed, as over 2 and under 4. Coarser mesh may be used occasionally if long strands will stay in place and wear satisfactorily. See page 42 for other weaving designs and the method of planning elaborate designs on squared paper.

The design you choose depends on:
    The size and shape of seat opening
    The width of splint you are using
    The number of warp strands and whether the
        number is even or uneven

Figure 4-12 shows weaving over 2 and under 3. Every other row is the same.

In Figure 4-13, weaving is also over 2 and under 3, but one warp strand to the left is used for each new row, creating a diagonal design. This design is used for the chair illustrated.

Weaving

Be sure the strand of splint is long enough to weave across the top of the seat and to join on the underside.

Loosen the last warp strand over the back rail, remove the clothespin, and bring the strand from the front under and over the back rail and under the preceding strand. Then bring the strand diagonally in front of the back post, under the side rail and turned so the right side is down (Figure 4-14).

Pull all strands tight and then weave across, right to left (Figure 4-15).

Pull the weaver over the side rail and weave the underside like the top, going over and under the same warp strands (Figure 4-16).

When you join pieces, staple from either side, if you know the staples will be hidden under warp strands (Figure 4-17). Or you can cover staples with short lengths of splint tucked under nearby strands.

Figure 4-18

Figure 4-19

Figure 4-20

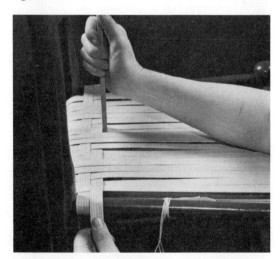

Figure 4-21

Figure 4-22

Figure 4-23

Figure 4-24

Flatten the sharp ends of staples with pliers, as before (Figure 4-18). Continue weaving, cutting the old strand inside the rail, even if you waste some of it, and forcing the joining in position. You cannot use the wrapper strand you tucked under until you get nearer the front (Figure 4-19).

The second row is over 2 and under 3 but one warp strand to the left of the first row (Figure 4-20). Or, weave to the right if you want the diagonal in the same direction as on the top of the seat.

Use a stick or a screwdriver to force the strands together. At the same time pull the strand across the rails so the seat will be firm (Figure 4-21).

On the underside, plan from near the center of the opening, where the pattern is established, how to begin the row and so continue the design used on the top (Figure 4-22). In this way you will weave over and under the same strands as you did on top.

When you have woven far enough to see the design, and have space, cut off a length of splint for a warp in the corner of the seat. Hook about 3 inches over the weaver strand which will continue the design, near the back of the seat (Figure 4-23). Or just push the strand in

Figure 4-25

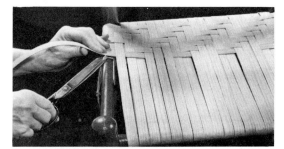
Figure 4-26

Figure 4-27

Figure 4-28

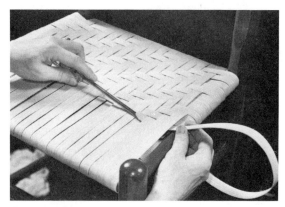
Figure 4-29

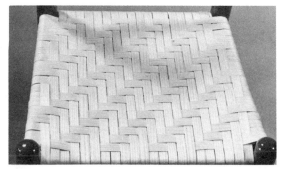
Figure 4-30

rather than hook it over a weaver, if it fits snugly.

Bring this warp strand to the underside of the seat and fasten there also (Figure 4-24).

Strands may be joined on top of the seat under the warp to save splint (Figure 4-25).

If the joining is secure, cut off the old strand so two thicknesses do not show. Also cut the string holding the first strand. Weaving holds this end in place (Figure 4-26).

Add other short lengths in the corners of the seat, as you have room for them (Figure 4-27).

Warp strands also are cut so ends are concealed. One or two staples and the weaving will hold the joining (Figure 4-28).

Use a screwdriver or similar blunt tool to help with weaving, as you get near the front of the seat (Figure 4-29).

Continue weaving to the front rail (Figure 4-30). Finish the underside by weaving as far across as you can and tuck the end under a warp strand (Figure 4-31).

If the back of the chair is to be woven, wrap strands the long way (up and down). Weave across from the bottom up so that you can push strands in place easily.

Figure 4-31

Figure 4-32

Figure 4-33

Figure 4-34

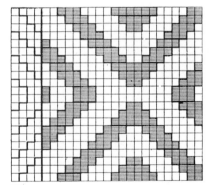

Figure 4-35

Figure 4-36

Figure 4-37

Other methods of joining splint

Figure 4-32 shows a more time-consuming method of joining splint. Notches are cut out and strands held together in the notch.

Splint joinings found on an old chair are shown in Figure 4-33. The arrow fits in the slotted end, holding the two securely.

Other weaving designs

The old rocker in Figure 4-34 has a pattern woven over 2 and under 2, creating a repeat pattern by using one strand to the left in each new row.

Elaborate designs are planned first on squared paper. Count the number of warp strands over the back rail. Estimate the number of rows from front to back by measuring with a piece of splint on one of the side rails. Allow one square on the paper for each strand across the back, and for each strand from back to front.

For a geometric design, choose as square an opening as possible or a design which can be adapted to a wider front rail. Begin in the center and work toward the sides and ends. The side sections indicate that the design can be continued if there is space for added rows (Figure 4-35).

WEAVING WITH OTHER MATERIALS

Flat reed

Flat reed is thinner and more pliable than splint and consequently is easier for beginners to use. It is not as smooth, as sturdy, or as fine a quality as splint. The right side of reed is smoother than the wrong side. Follow the directions for weaving splint seats.

The seat in Figure 4-36 is woven with 3/8-inch flat reed, stained to blend with the paint on the chair frame. The design was first drawn on squared paper. The uneven number of strands across the back (29) and the simple lines of the chair permit a geometric design planned from the center to the sides. The width of strand must also be checked on the side rail to be sure there is space to complete the design; there are 30 strands over these rails.

Flat oval reed

Flat oval reed is used mostly for porch furniture. The right side is beveled and the other is flat. Strands can be

Figure 4-38

Figure 4-39

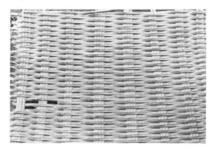

Figure 4-40

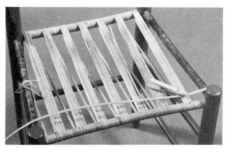

Figure 4-41

Figure 4-42

Figure 4-43

rolled smaller than splint, to fit in a bowl about 11 inches in diameter for soaking.

The seat in Figure 4-37 is made of wide (3/8-inch) flat oval reed, woven over 4 and under 4 in a diagonal design. With 34 warp strands over the back rail, the first strand was woven under 3 on each side, to start the design. A smaller pattern is not desirable because this reed is thick and would be hard to force in place. Weaving is easier if warp strands are a little slack. Corner strands, 3 on each side, were filled in as there was space and the pattern became established, counting four each way each row. The design is woven on the underside also (Figure 4-38).

Figure 4-39 shows a section of an old seat woven with 3/16-inch flat oval reed. The design on the top is over 4 and under 4, in a zigzag pattern. With room on the side rails for about 54 weaver strands, the design was planned for 4 repeats of 12 each, with 3 additional rows for the points, and weavers added to fill the space at the front and back.

Three or four strands may be used together for warping as in the section of old seat shown in Figure 4-40. Weaving is over and under warp strands, alternating each row.

Wide binding cane

Wide binding cane is also used for outdoor furniture. Strands are about 3/16 inch wide; the right side is glossy and smooth but with frequent "eyes" or joints. Be careful to weave with these joints rather than roughen or break them; discard poor strands. Strands can be rolled to fit in a bowl 6 inches in diameter.

The chair in Figure 4-41 shows warping back to front and will be woven side to side.

Staple the first strand to the left side rail. Pull the strand to the front rail and wind around (over and under) this rail 5 times. Continue the strand to the back rail and wrap around it and the front rail 3 times. Wrap around the front rail 5 times and pull the strand to the back rail, close to the previous strand. Wrap around the back rail 5 times, and continue the design until you fill the back rail. Finish by wrapping around the front rail 5 times and continue this strand to start weaving. The top of the finished seat (Figure 4-42) shows the design woven over and under the groups of warp strands, alternating each row. Warp strands are straight from

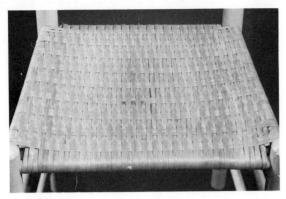

Figure 4-44

front to back on top of the seat, but on the bottom, one of the grouping of 3 has to be diagonal near the back rail (Figure 4-43).

Note that weaving from side to side leaves spaces at the front of the seat.

The seat shown in Figure 4-44 avoids spaces at the front by warping side to side, and weaving back to front. Note that the corners on the top are filled with short strands; ends might be bent, tucked in, and stapled to a strand on the underside of the seat.

HOW TO FINISH THE SEAT

Trim off hairs or rough places with a razor blade or knife. Splint that has a hard glossy surface needs no finish. However if you want the seat to blend with the color of the chair, apply one or more coats of blending seat stain, available from dealers of seating supplies. Varnish finishes generally dry materials and cause them to split and crack. Penetrating oil stains that color and seal or polyurethane finishes are preferable. Let the seat dry thoroughly and then apply 2 or 3 thin coats to both sides of the seat. Dry thoroughly between coats.

Reed has little natural finish; a polyurethane finish or an oil stain and sealer may be used.